Smithsonian

TIMELINE SCIENCE:

SPACE
EXPLORATION

Silver Dolphin

Silver Dolphin Books
An imprint of Printers Row Publishing Group
10350 Barnes Canyon Road, Suite 100, San Diego, CA 92121
www.silverdolphinbooks.com

ISBN: 978-1-62686-947-9

Manufactured, printed, and assembled in China.
21 20 19 18 17 1 2 3 4 5

Written by Megan Roth
Designed by Dynamo Limited

For Smithsonian Enterprises:
Chris Liedel, President
Carol LeBlanc, Senior Vice President, Education and Consumer Products
Brigid Ferraro, Vice President, Education and Consumer Products
Ellen Nanney, Licensing Manager
Kealy Gordon, Product Development Manager, Licensing
Reviewed by Valerie Neal, Curator and Chair, Space History Department, National Air and Space Museum, Smithsonian.

Image Credits:
Images copyright Thinkstock, Superstock, Inc., Shutterstock, Smithsonian Institution, NASA.

Every effort has been made to contact copyright holders for the images in this book. If you are the copyright holder of any uncredited image herein, please contact us at Silver Dolphin Books, 10350 Barnes Canyon Road, Suite 100, San Diego, CA 92121.

CONTENTS

INTRODUCTION TO SPACE EXPLORATION

When the Sun begins to set, and the Moon and stars appear in the night sky, you're looking at a part of space. The universe, or all of space, is an incredibly huge, wide-open area that holds everything that can be measured or touched. Whether it's stars, galaxies, planets, or even you, they're all part of the universe.

Nicolaus Copernicus

It wasn't until 1543 that Nicolaus Copernicus, a Polish astronomer, suggested that Earth actually revolved around the Sun. During Copernicus's time, astronomers believed Ptolomy's theory from 1,000 years earlier. Ptolomy was a Greek astronomer who believed that Earth was the center of the universe. Copernicus, however, questioned this belief and began thinking that the planets revolved around the Sun. By the 1600s, Galileo verified Copernicus's theory and thus changed the way people thought about Earth and its relationship to the Sun and other planets.

Much has changed since the time of Copernicus and Galileo. It was only in 1961 that the first human was sent into space to orbit Earth. Today, explorers continue to venture into space searching for new discoveries. Robots, rovers, and new technology are being used to learn about the far reaches of the universe. In the 500 years since the first astronomer changed the way we think about the universe, we have learned amazing things about the planet we live on. The universe is full of other planets, solar systems, and galaxies, all just waiting to be explored.

OUR SOLAR SYSTEM

Our solar system is about 4.6 billion years old and is made up of eight planets. Four planets are terrestrial and four are gas giants. Mercury, Venus, Earth, and Mars are the closest to the Sun and have a rocky, solid surface. Jupiter, Saturn, Uranus, and Neptune are farther away from the Sun and consist of gases. The Sun is the center of our solar system and is so big its gravity pulls everything in the solar system towards it.

Earth is the only planet in our solar system known to have life.

Earth

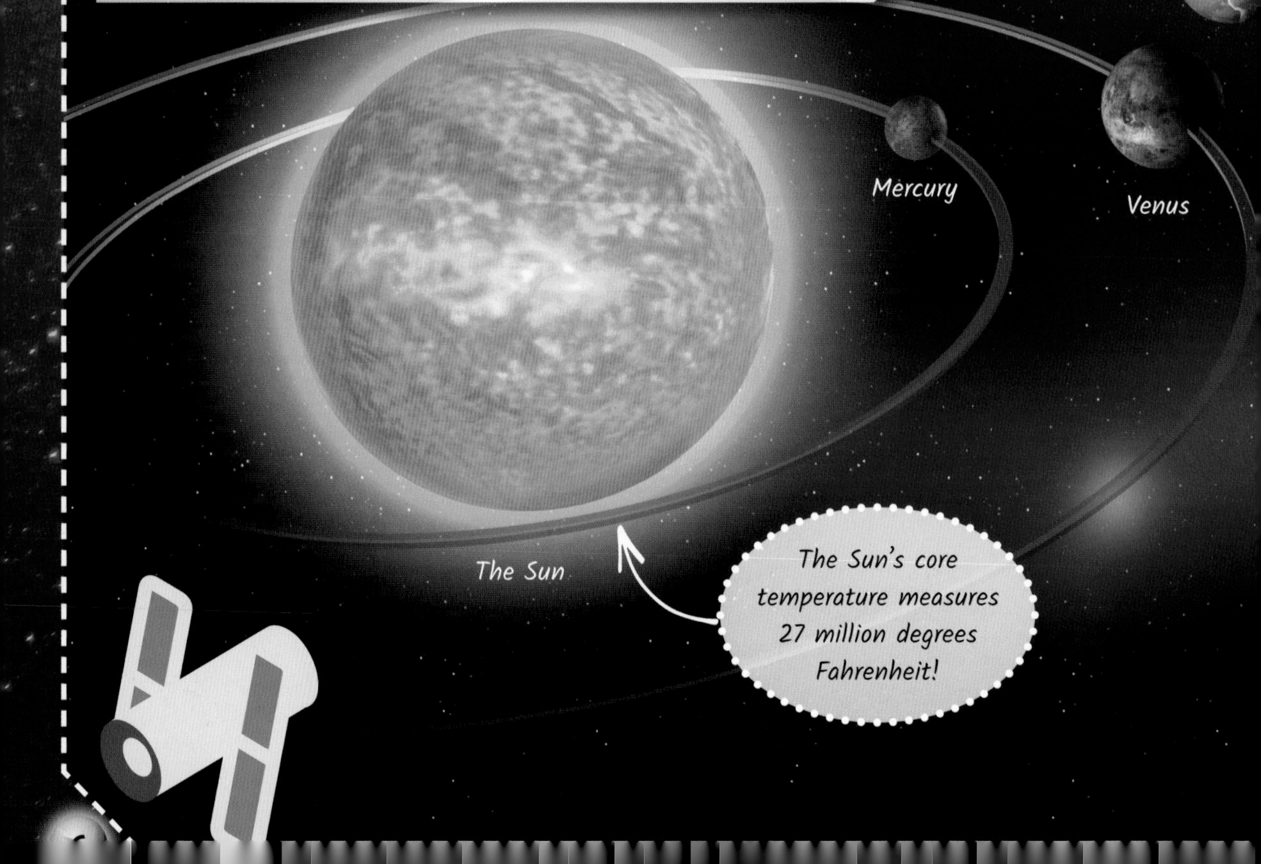

Mercury

Venus

The Sun

The Sun's core temperature measures 27 million degrees Fahrenheit!

Neptune

Saturn

Jupiter

Uranus

Mars

In 1610, Italian astronomer Galileo Galilei looked at Saturn through a telescope and noticed strange objects, which he described as "arms," on each side of it. Hundreds of years later, scientists discovered that the "arms" were actually its rings.

Our solar system orbits around one star, but there are billions of stars in one galaxy, and there may even be hundreds of billions of galaxies in our universe.

THE SUN

The Sun is the star at the center of our solar system and accounts for 99.86 percent of our solar system's mass. It is so gigantic that 1.3 million Earths could fit inside it! It is billions of years old and will continue burning for billions of years to come.

The Sun is made of gas and the same elements found in planets. The planets, dwarf planets, asteroids, comets, and meteoroids were made from what was left over after the Sun formed.

MERCURY

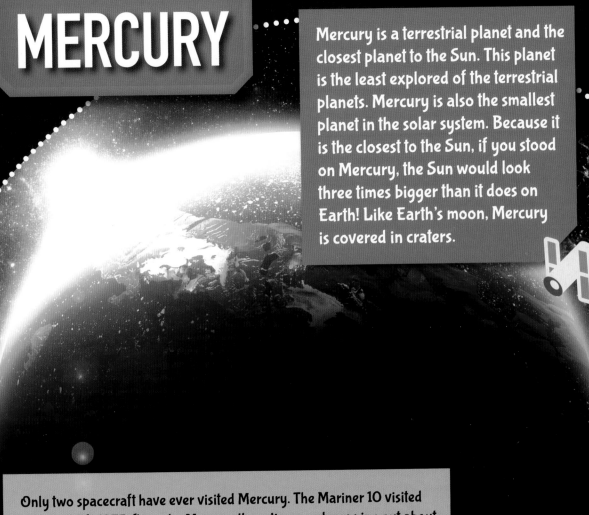

Mercury is a terrestrial planet and the closest planet to the Sun. This planet is the least explored of the terrestrial planets. Mercury is also the smallest planet in the solar system. Because it is the closest to the Sun, if you stood on Mercury, the Sun would look three times bigger than it does on Earth! Like Earth's moon, Mercury is covered in craters.

Only two spacecraft have ever visited Mercury. The Mariner 10 visited during 1974–1975, flying by Mercury three times and mapping out about half of its surface. On March 24, 1975, the Mariner 10 ran out of fuel and is still believed to be orbiting the Sun. The Messenger probe was launched in 2004 to explore more of Mercury, including its density, geological history, and magnetic field.

Mercury's temperatures swing from being extremely hot during the day to bitterly cold at night. The side facing away from the Sun has close to the coldest temperatures in the solar system. Although helium, oxygen, and sodium exist on the planet's surface, strong winds send these gases out to space, so Mercury is pretty much airless.

VENUS

Venus is the second planet from the Sun and the closest planet to Earth. Venus and Earth are sometimes referred to as twins because they are similar in terms of materials, size, and mass. But unlike on Earth, life on Venus would be impossible. It is scorching hot, and the air is full of deadly acid. Sulfuric acid on the planet smells like rotten eggs!

Venus rotates in reverse, meaning the Sun rises in the west and sets in the east. Because of the way its clouds reflect sunlight, Venus is the brightest-looking planet in the sky. It is sometimes called the Morning and Evening Star.

The ancient Romans thought Venus was one of four planets in our solar system other than Earth. As the brightest of the visible planets, Venus was named after the Romans' goddess of love and beauty.

EARTH

Earth, the planet we call home, was formed around 4.6 billion years ago and is the only known planet to support life. Earth is the third planet from the Sun and is home to more than 30 million different forms of life.

Earth is made up of four layers. The crust is the top layer and the layer we live on. Oceans cover about 70 percent of Earth's surface, which is why photos taken from space show Earth as looking mostly blue. The mantle is right under the crust and is very hot, dense rock that flows like liquid asphalt. Under the mantle sits the outer core, which is made from metals such as nickel and iron. The outer core is so hot that these metals are liquid. Finally, the inner core is Earth's center. It is so hot, 9,800°F, that the metals are squeezed together into a solid.

EARTH'S MOON

Moons are natural objects that orbit planets, thanks to gravity. Some planets, like Jupiter, have many moons, and some, like Earth, only have one. Astronomers believe that a very long time ago, Earth smashed into an object the size of Mars. The collision broke off huge chunks of Earth that were flung into space. Over time, Earth chunks joined and made our Moon.

If you were to travel to the Moon today, you'd see the footprints of the first astronauts to land there in 1969. That's because there is no weathering from wind or rain. They will still be on the Moon's surface millions of years from now.

Only 12 people have ever walked on the Moon. Starting with Neil Armstrong in 1969 and ending with Gene Cernan in 1972. All other lunar missions have been un-piloted spacecraft, but NASA has plans to set up a permanent space station on the Moon.

MARS

Mars is the fourth planet from the Sun and the last of the terrestrial planets. Sometimes Mars is referred to as the "Red Planet" because it has a red surface color. Similar to Earth, Mars has deserts, canyons, and frozen north and south poles. Scientists are particularly interested in Mars because they believe it was once similar to Earth!

Mariner 4, launched in 1964, successfully flew by Mars and got a close look at the planet. In 1976, Viking 1 and Viking 2 were the first spacecraft to actually land on Mars. Both spacecraft collected photos and samples from the planet and conducted biological tests to look for possible signs of life. In January 2004, the rovers, or robotic, un-piloted spacecraft, *Spirit* and *Opportunity*, landed on Mars and cruised around the planet capturing stunning images of the Martian landscape. The rovers also gathered important evidence that suggests that the planet may have been wet and livable at one point.

In 2012, NASA successfully landed the Curiosity Rover that started to perform research. Today, scientists search the planet using the latest technology to look for signs of life. Perhaps more importantly, they are also mapping any environmental hazards for future piloted missions to Mars.

JUPITER

Jupiter is the fifth planet from the Sun and the first of the gas giants. It also happens to be the largest planet in our solar system. Galileo was the first to observe four of Jupiter's moons in 1610, which proved that celestial bodies orbited planets other than Earth.

Unlike Earth, which only has one moon, Jupiter holds the record of having the most moons—at least 67! Because it does not have a solid surface like the terrestrial planets, astronauts would not be able to land on Jupiter, but there have been spacecraft and probes that have flown near the gas giant.

Jupiter is often referred to as the solar system's vacuum cleaner because its massive gravitational pull sucks in nearby comets and meteors. The Great Red Spot is a massive storm that has been raging on Jupiter for more than 500 years! It once measured 25,000 miles in diameter. Now it's only a bit bigger than Earth at just less than 10,000 miles in diameter. Because there is not an underlying landmass, scientists believe that the storms on Jupiter will continue to happen.

SATURN

Saturn is the sixth planet from the Sun and one of the most recognizable planets because of its rings. Often referred to as "The Ringed Planet," Saturn has seven rings, which are icy and made up of dust and rock pieces.

Saturn is the farthest planet that we can see from Earth with unaided eyes, but the planet has been visited by spacecraft. The Pioneer 11 mission first visited Saturn in 1979 and a number of photos of the planet were taken. Then, in 1980 and 1981, twin Voyagers were sent to gather even more information. In 2004, Cassini–Huygens entered Saturn's orbit and remains there to this day, sending back information about the planet.

URANUS

On March 13, 1781, Sir William Hershel, a British astronomer, discovered Uranus. Without the aid of a telescope, the planet was hard to detect. In fact, Hershel first believed the planet was a comet, but years later, discovered that the object's orbit was circular and not elliptical like a comet's orbit. Thanks to a telescope he constructed, Hershel's discovery of Uranus became the first in modern history.

The planet's most unusual feature is its orientation. Rather than rotating like the other planets in our solar system, Uranus rotates on its side, with its rings and moons orbiting in a bull's-eye pattern.

When viewed through a telescope, Uranus looks a bit like a glowing green pea. The planet is often referred to as the "Ice Giant" because the methane gas and ice crystals in Uranus's atmosphere cause a blue-green coloring.

Saturn is not the only planet in our solar system with rings—Uranus has rings, too! In 1977, scientists first spotted a band of rings around Uranus. Today, 15 rings have been discovered. Compared to Saturn's rings, the rings around Uranus are narrow and dark.

Today, only one spacecraft has flown by Uranus. In 1986, the Voyager 2 probe flew past the planet and took close-up images of the planet's atmosphere, moons, and ring system.

NEPTUNE

Neptune is the eighth planet from the Sun and the last of the known planets. Jean Joseph Le Verrier and John Couch Adams discovered the planet, but there is often debate on who should be credited for its discovery. Neptune was the first planet discovered through mathematics instead of observation. Shortly after the discovery of the planet Uranus, astronomers observed that the planet was orbiting in a way that suggested another major body in our solar system was influencing it.

OBSERVATION

In 1845, John Couch Adams calculated the position of the unknown planet that had a gravitational field close to Uranus. He submitted his findings to the Royal Society in England, but they went unnoticed. A year later, Le Verrier submitted similar calculations and the scientific community finally took notice. On September 23, 1846, an astronomer named Johann Gall observed the planet near Adam's calculations but even closer to Le Verrier's. Today, most scientists credit both men with the discovery of Neptune.

Only one spacecraft has flown past Neptune. In 1989, the Voyager 2 captured the first close-up images of the planet and was sent to examine Triton, the largest of Neptune's moons. It took over four hours for signals from the probe to reach Earth. Images from the probe featured a "Great Dark Spot" similar to Jupiter's "Great Red Spot," showing that the climate is active on the planet and has high-speed winds that can reach a speed of 1,500 miles per hour!

DWARF PLANETS & PLUTO

Dwarf planets are round bodies like planets but much smaller. Five dwarf planets have been named, but there are likely more in our solar system that have yet to be discovered.

DWARF PLANETS

Ceres, Pluto, Haumea, Makemake, and Eris are the dwarf planets in our solar system. In 2006, the characteristics of a dwarf planet were redefined. If a celestial body has the following characteristics, it is considered a dwarf planet:

- It orbits around the Sun
- Has sufficient mass for its self-gravity to overcome rigid body forces so that it assumes a nearly round shape
- Has not cleared the neighborhood around its orbit, meaning that, like Pluto, a dwarf planet crosses another planet's path in orbit
- Is not a satellite (moon)

In 1930, Clyde Tombaugh, an American astronomer, discovered Pluto in our solar system, and it was considered the ninth planet. However, in 2006, it was redefined as a dwarf planet. Pluto is located in the Kuiper Belt, a disk-shaped region beyond Neptune's orbit.

In 2015, the *New Horizons* mission flew by Pluto to capture the first high-resolution photographs of the dwarf planet. The spacecraft mission was launched in 2005 to study Pluto and the other icy objects in the Kuiper Belt.

THE STARS

When you look up on a clear night and see tiny specks of light in the sky, you're actually looking at enormous stars. Stars are hot balls of gas that burn for billions of years. On Earth, the closest star is the Sun, which is roughly 93 million miles away.

The universe is made up of spinning galaxies that are made up of millions of stars and systems made up of planets, comets, asteroids, and other space objects that orbit a single star. We live in a system of planets located in the Milky Way Galaxy. The Milky Way contains hundreds of billions of stars—our Sun included.

Our solar system orbits around this one star, but there can be billions of stars in one galaxy and there may even be billions of galaxies in our universe! Up until 1920, most astronomers believed that all of the stars were contained inside the Milky Way, but an American astronomer named Edwin Hubble proved that the Milky Way is actually just one of billions of galaxies in the universe.

The Milky Way

INTRODUCTION TO SPACE TRAVEL & EXPLORATION

Humans have been staring up at the stars and planets since they first walked on Earth. It wasn't until 500 years ago that the first astronomer proposed that Earth rotated and revolved around the Sun. It wasn't until 1961 that the first human was sent into space to orbit Earth, and it wasn't until 1969 that the first human stepped on the Moon. Our knowledge and understanding of the planets around us and the universe that we are a part of has only increased since we have developed new technologies to explore these unknown places.

Right now, there are spacecraft snapping photos, collecting data, and conducting tests, further illuminating the mysteries of our solar system and beyond. Since the 1960s, a variety of different spacecraft have been sent into space; some of them extend the range of what astronauts can do there.

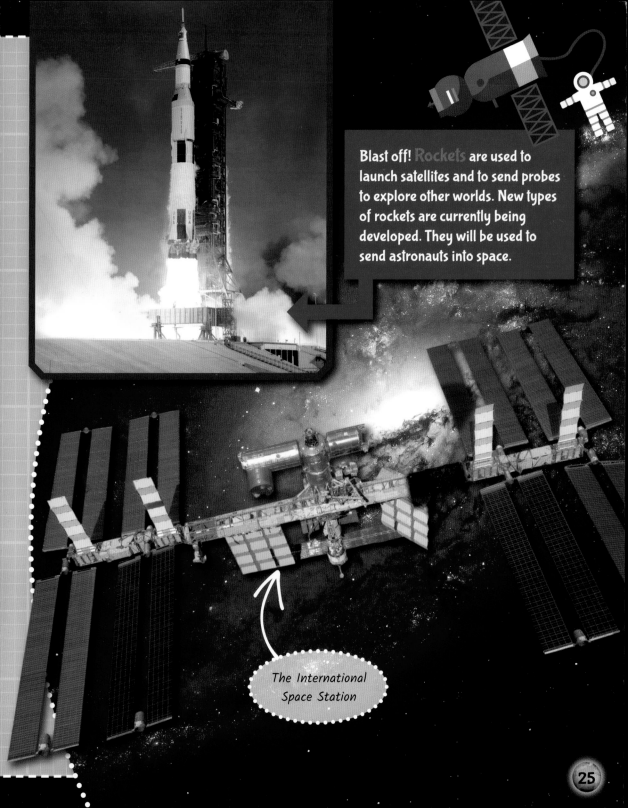

Blast off! Rockets are used to launch satellites and to send probes to explore other worlds. New types of rockets are currently being developed. They will be used to send astronauts into space.

The International Space Station

THE BEGINNING OF THE SPACE RACE: 1957-1960

The Space Race was a competition between the United States and the Soviet Union. Between 1957 and 1975, both countries used their groundbreaking technology to prove superiority in space exploration.

The United States and the Soviet Union were both experimenting with satellites. During the Cold War, the public believed these satellites would be used for purely scientific efforts, but both countries understood that an orbiting satellite could also help them observe any ground attacks from above.

The Soviet Union launched their satellite first. On October 4, 1957, they launched *Sputnik 1*, the world's first satellite and first machine-produced object to be placed in Earth's orbit. It was a metal ball, 23 inches across, and weighed about 184 pounds. A transmitter inside the satellite sent out signals that could be picked up by radios on Earth.

THE BEGINNING OF THE SPACE RACE: 1957-1960

Just a month after *Sputnik 1* was launched, the Soviet Union sent *Sputnik 2* into orbit. This new satellite carried the first living creature into space—a dog named Laika. The flight was meant to test the safety of space travel for humans, but unfortunately technology was not ready, and Laika did not make the return trip back to Earth.

In the United States, space was already being seen as the next step for exploration, and they didn't want to fall behind the Russians. In January 1958, the United States had their first success with the launch of a satellite called the *Explorer 1*. It was designed by the US Army under the direction of a rocket scientist named Wernher von Braun.

In July of that year, President Dwight Eisenhower announced the creation of the National Aeronautics and Space Administration, or NASA, a federal agency dedicated to space exploration. This emphasized the United States' dedication in winning the Space Race.

EISENHOWER·USA

8c

By 1959, both countries had a new goal: sending staffed missions to the Moon. The Soviets launched *Luna 1* in January, but it missed its target and instead became the first spacecraft to orbit the Sun. In March, the United States launched *Pioneer 4*, which also missed the Moon. Finally, the Soviet Union took a step forward in space exploration with the launch of *Luna 9*, which became the first space probe to land on the Moon.

THE BEGINNING OF THE SPACE RACE: 1961-1966

On April 12, 1961, the Soviet Union made another big step in space history when cosmonaut Yuri Gagarin became the first person to orbit Earth, traveling in a capsule-like spacecraft called *Vostok 1*. He successfully made one complete orbit around Earth. Nearing the end of its orbit, Gagarin's spacecraft began spinning out of control, but this was not made public until decades after the landing.

Yuri Gagarin

PROJECT MERCURY

Meanwhile the United States was actively making efforts to send a man into space. Called Project Mercury, NASA engineers designed a cone-shaped capsule and tested the spacecraft with chimpanzees. On the morning of January 31, 1961, a 5-year-old chimpanzee named Ham boarded a NASA capsule and became the first chimp in space. His 16-minute suborbital mission led to the United States making necessary revisions to next put a person into the Mercury capsule.

On May 5, astronaut Alan Shepard became the first American in space, although he did not finish a complete orbit. He named his spacecraft *Freedom 7*. The flight only lasted 15 minutes.

The "Mercury Seven" was a group of seven carefully selected astronauts that worked on staffed spaceflights during the program from May 1961 to May 1963. The seven original American astronauts were Scott Carpenter, Gordon Cooper, John Glenn, Gus Grissom, Wally Schirra, Alan Shepard, and Deke Slayton. The success of the Mercury Seven's flights proved that human spaceflight was possible and paved the way for future space missions.

John Glenn

AIR MAIL
3 RIYALS

GEMINI

JOHN F. KENNEDY
MAY 29th, 1917

AJMAN عجمان

President John F. Kennedy made space exploration a priority when he was in office. In May 1961, he claimed that the United States would land a man on the Moon before the end of the decade. Luckily, they were on their way. In February 1962, John Glenn became the first American to orbit Earth. NASA's lunar landing program was in place and the United States was ready to send a man to the Moon! From 1961 to 1964, NASA's budget increased almost 500 percent to aid in the lunar landing program.

THE BEGINNING OF THE SPACE RACE: 1961-1966

While the United States was getting ready for a trip to the Moon, the Soviet Union had another milestone in their space program. In June 1963, aboard the *Vostok 6*, Soviet Cosmonaut Valentina Tereshkova became the first woman to travel into space. After 48 orbits and 71 hours, she returned to Earth, having spent more time in space than all US astronauts combined at the time.

PROJECT GEMINI

Project Gemini, consisting of Gemini 9 and 10, was another early NASA program, started shortly after Project Mercury. These two missions helped prepare the United States for the Apollo program. In Project Gemini, ten crews flew in 1965 and 1966. The Gemini spacecraft, unlike Mercury, could hold two people instead of one. With this program, NASA learned that astronauts could go outside a spacecraft in a space suit. The Gemini 9 mission tested different ways spacecraft could fly near one another, and the Gemini 10 mission connected one spacecraft with another spacecraft and used its engine to move both vehicles. All of these things had to be learned before NASA could successfully land an astronaut on the Moon.

THE APOLLO PROGRAM

The Apollo program was designed by NASA to land humans on the Moon and bring them back to Earth safely. Some of the flights tested the spacecraft and looked at other components. Six of the seven missions successfully landed on the Moon (Apollo 11, 12, 14, 15, 16, and 17) and brought back important scientific data and lunar samples. Unfortunately, Apollo 13 malfunctioned.

APOLLO 1

On January 27, 1967, tragedy struck during preflight test for AS–204. The mission was to be the first Apollo flight and was scheduled to launch in February, but Astronauts Virgil Grissom, Edward White, and Roger Chaffee lost their lives when a fire swept through the command module. In the spring of 1967, NASA's Associate Administrator for Manned Space Flight, Dr. George E. Muller, announced that the mission would be known as Apollo 1.

APOLLO 8

On Christmas Eve in 1968, millions watched and listened as the Apollo 8 astronauts took off for the Moon. Apollo 8 became the first mission to take humans to the Moon and back. Before humans could actually land on the Moon, NASA wanted to test the flight path and spacecraft operations. Launching with the Saturn V, the Apollo 8 pilots were the first humans to take pictures of Earth from deep space.

APOLLO 10

The Apollo 10 mission was a complete staging of the Apollo 11 mission without actually landing on the Moon. The liftoff marked the fourth staffed Apollo launch in just seven months.

THE APOLLO PROGRAM

APOLLO 11

The Saturn V rocket launches Apollo 11 mission from Kennedy Space Center.

The main objective of Apollo 11 was to complete the national goal set by President John F. Kennedy on May 25, 1961: to perform a lunar landing by the end of the decade. On July 20, 1969, the first lunar landing mission was a success. Commander Neil Armstrong, Lunar Module Pilot Edwin "Buzz" Aldrin, and Command Module Pilot Michael Collins performed scientific experiments on the Moon's surface, took photographs of the lunar terrain, and brought soil and rock samples back to Earth. An estimated 530 million people watched Armstrong's television image and heard his voice describe the event as he took "one small step for a man, one giant leap for mankind."

Taking off on July 16, 1969, the astronauts took three days to finally arrive on the Moon. Then on July 20, Neil Armstrong and Buzz Aldrin became the first humans to set foot on the Moon. Michael Collins remained in orbit around the Moon waiting for his fellow astronauts to rejoin him. Aldrin and Armstrong planted an American flag on the Moon along with a commemorative plaque, and, of course, their footprints!

APOLLO 12 "THE PINPOINT MISSION"

The second staffed mission to land on the Moon was planned and executed to be a precision landing and to perform scientific exploration. The astronauts landed the Lunar Module within walking distance to the Surveyor III spacecraft that landed on the Moon in April 1967. The astronauts brought back instruments from the Surveyor III to examine the effects of long-term exposure to a lunar environment. The landing was important because it meant that landing points in rough terrain could be targeted and explored.

pollo 11 display at the Smithsonian.

HERE MEN FROM THE PLANET EARTH
FIRST SET FOOT UPON THE MOON
JULY 1969, A. D.
WE CAME IN PEACE FOR ALL MANKIND

NEIL A. ARMSTRONG
ASTRONAUT

MICHAEL COLLINS
ASTRONAUT

EDWIN E. ALDRIN, JR.
ASTRONAUT

RICHARD NIXON
PRESIDENT, UNITED STATES OF AMERICA

THE APOLLO PROGRAM

APOLLO 13

"Houston, we've had a problem."

On April 11, 1970, Apollo 13 launched from Kennedy Space Center. The mission was planned as a lunar landing mission but was aborted en route to the Moon after just 56 hours of flight because they lost connection to their oxygen and the capability to produce water. The explosion crippled the spacecraft, and the crew was forced to orbit the Moon, instead of landing on it.

APOLLO 14

In 1971, the Apollo 14 mission was the third staffed lunar landing mission. Its objective and destination was the same as the aborted Apollo 13 mission. A color television camera mounted on the descent stage provided live coverage of the descent of both astronauts to the lunar surface. They collected samples and took photographs by a nearby crater. One of the most famous moments of the Apollo 14 mission was when commander Alan Shepard hit two golf balls on the Moon!

Lunar Rover

APOLLO 15

This mission was the debut of the lunar roving vehicle used to explore the geology of the Hadley–Apennine region, a region on the near side of the Moon bordered by a mountain range and a zigzag channel.

APOLLO 17

Apollo 17 was the last Apollo mission to land astronauts on the Moon. Eugene Cernan, commander of Apollo 17, still holds the distinction of being the last person to walk on the Moon. No humans have visited the Moon since December 14, 1972, because NASA's goal has changed since then. Today, NASA's focus has shifted to humans staying on the Moon for longer periods of time. NASA is working on creating new tools and technologies to construct semi–permanent habitats on the lunar surface.

APOLLO 16

Apollo 16 landed in a highlands area, a region that had not been explored yet. Astronauts collected samples, took photographs, and conducted experiments that included the first use of a UV camera/spectrograph on the Moon.

SKYLAB

The United States first space station was called Skylab. Rocco Petrone, engineer and former director of NASA's Marshall Space Flight Center, launched Skylab out of NASA's Kennedy Space Center during 1973 and 1974. The project began as the Apollo Applications Program in 1968 to help develop space missions to successfully land humans on the Moon. The last mission of the Saturn V rocket, which is famous for the Moon landing, was the launch of Skylab.

Skylab orbited Earth from 1973 to 1979. It was a 169,950-pound space station that had a workshop, a solar observatory, a docking adapter, and systems that allowed crews to stay in space for up to 84 days. After slight delays in liftoff with Skylab 1, the Skylab 2 crew made a few necessary adjustments and focused on studying microgravity, observing Earth from the sky, researching solar astronomy, and proving that humans could be in space for longer periods of time.

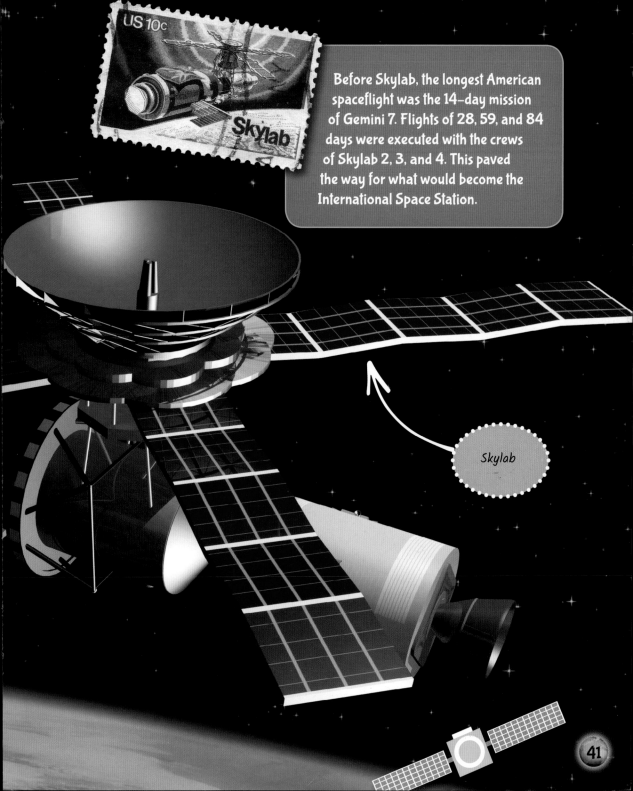

US 10c

Skylab

Before Skylab, the longest American spaceflight was the 14-day mission of Gemini 7. Flights of 28, 59, and 84 days were executed with the crews of Skylab 2, 3, and 4. This paved the way for what would become the International Space Station.

Skylab

VOYAGER 1 & VOYAGER 2

Voyager 1 and 2 are currently exploring places in the galaxy that no other probe has explored! The Voyager twin spacecraft will be the third and fourth spacecraft to fly beyond all the planets in our solar system. Pioneers 10 and 11 were the first two probes, but in February 1998 the Voyager 1 passed Pioneer 10.

Voyager 1 launched on September 5, 1977 about two weeks before its twin, Voyager 2. Together, the two probes conducted a grand tour of the gas giants, giving scientists some of their first up–close looks at Jupiter, Saturn, Uranus, Neptune, and the moons of these faraway planets. After initially being sent to explore active volcanoes on Jupiter's moon Io and learning more about the rings of Saturn, their mission was extended. The twins completed their primary mission in 1989 and then kept flying to the edge of the heliosphere. Voyager 2 went on to explore Uranus and Neptune, and is still the only spacecraft to have visited those outer planets.

Voyager

After traveling through space for more than 35 years, NASA's robotic Voyager 1 probe left the solar system in August 2012 making a historic entry into interstellar space. Scientists hope to learn more about this region when Voyager 2 also reaches interstellar space. Both probes are still sending scientific information about their surroundings through the Deep Space Network, a worldwide network of antennas and communication facilities that support spacecraft missions.

THE SPACE SHUTTLE ERA

NASA's Space Shuttle, a partially reusable low-orbit spacecraft, first launched on April 12, 1981, and retired on July 21, 2011. The Space Shuttle was made up of three main parts: the orbiter, the external tank, and rocket boosters. The fleet of orbiters included *Columbia*, *Challenger*, *Discovery*, *Atlantis*, and *Endeavor*. Together, they flew 135 missions, took satellites to space so they could orbit Earth, and helped build the International Space Station.

FUN FACT

The Space Shuttle was originally going to be called *Constitution*, but as the Shuttle was being developed, *Star Trek* fans organized a campaign and sent letters to the White House asking for the name to be *Enterprise*.

The first Space Shuttle never actually made it to space. The *Enterprise* was built without engines or a heat shield and was not capable of spaceflight. Instead, they used it as a test vehicle. It tested landing phases and shuttle preparations. The *Enterprise* was used in "drop tests" in California to let astronauts get an idea for how the Shuttle would fly during its descent back to Earth.

In 1981, *Columbia* was the first Shuttle to reach space. The Shuttle program was officially called the Space Transportation System (STS), so the first mission was known as STS-1. It was the first time in history a spacecraft was launched on its first voyage with a crew aboard.

In the two decades that *Columbia* flew, it reached several important milestones, including microgravity laboratory missions, operating the robotic arm, and experimenting with a tethered satellite system. However, the Shuttle and a seven-member crew were lost over Texas when *Columbia* burned up during re-entry in 2003. The loss made NASA perform extra safety checks in orbit on all future missions.

THE SPACE SHUTTLE ERA

CHALLENGER

The next Space Shuttle, called *Challenger*, was one of NASA's greatest triumphs, and it was the second Shuttle to reach space in April 1983. It completed nine milestone missions, including spacewalks and the use of a robotic arm in space.

The first successful launch of *Challenger* also marked the release of the first Tracking and Data Relay Satellite, which let astronauts stay in touch with controllers back home.

Astronauts Story Musgrave and Donald Peterson also did the first spacewalk on the Shuttle program. *Challenger* was also the first operational Spacelab flight. In April 1984, astronaut George Nelson strapped himself into the Manned Maneuvering Unit, a jet–powered backpack, to fly into space. Nelson flew over to a satellite, fixed it, and then returned it to service using the robotic arm.

Even with its successes, *Challenger* was also the reason for one of NASA's darkest moments. On its tenth launch into space, in 1986, the Shuttle exploded just 73 seconds after liftoff, killing all seven of its crew members. Every January, NASA remembers the last crew of *Challenger*, and the other crews lost in space exploration, on a NASA Day of Remembrance.

FUN FACT

On June 18, 1983, Sally Ride became the first American woman to fly in space when the Space Shuttle *Challenger* launched during mission STS-7. The first African American, Guion Bluford, reached space on STS-8.

DISCOVERY

In 1984, the Space Shuttle *Discovery* launched into space.

Until 2011, when the space program ended, *Discovery* flew more missions than any other Space Shuttle—flying 39 times! *Discovery* has played an important role in space exploration and is particularly noteworthy for doing both "return to flight" missions after the *Challenger* and *Columbia* accidents.

In 1990, the Hubble Space Telescope was launched from *Discovery*. From the *Discovery's* windows and cargo bay, stunning photos of Earth have been captured. *Discovery* also sent the Ulysses spacecraft to study the Sun and helped build the International Space Station.

FUN FACT

In 2008, the crew aboard *Discovery* brought a Buzz Lightyear toy to the International Space Station (ISS). He lived on the ISS until 2009 when the *Discovery* brought him back to Earth.

THE SPACE SHUTTLE ERA

ATLANTIS

Atlantis made its first flight on October 3, 1985, and was the last one to fly into space. It performed for more than 25 years and completed 33 missions. The Shuttle sent many satellites into space and also served as the final Shuttle to service the Hubble Space Telescope. On *Atlantis's* fourth flight, NASA had another historic first. On board the Shuttle was Magellan, a spacecraft that would be launched toward Venus. *Atlantis* repeated this historic feat when it sent another probe toward Jupiter.

In the mid 1990s, *Atlantis's* focus changed when NASA and Russia made a deal for American astronauts to stay aboard the Russian Space Station Mir in return for crew rotation and delivery of various supplies and equipment. The two countries created an international agreement on human space flight, and astronauts and cosmonauts began to work together on research.

NASA flew 11 missions to Mir and the *Atlantis* did most of those flights. The Shuttle flew seven times in a row bringing astronauts back and forth. When *Atlantis* and Mir were hooked together, they formed the largest spacecraft orbiting Earth at the time.

ENDEAVOUR

Endeavour was the fifth and final space shuttle to be built in the Space Shuttle Era and was built right after the program's greatest tragedy, the *Challenger* explosion. NASA ran a competition in US schools to name the next shuttle. About 6,000 schools participated in the contest and about one-third of schools chose the name *Endeavour*. The *Endeavour* was a British ship that was best known for its first voyage where James Cook brought the ship to Tahiti to watch the transit of Venus across the Sun.

The *Endeavour* flew into space 25 times and had many career highlights. *Endeavour*'s crew performed a Hubble Space Telescope servicing mission, which repaired the telescope's faulty mirror and installed solar panels. The December 1993 mission also had five spacewalks in five days.

HUBBLE SPACE TELESCOPE

In 1990, NASA launched one of the most powerful telescopes yet—the Hubble Space Telescope. Unlike telescopes on the ground, the Hubble Space Telescope orbits above Earth's atmosphere. Its astonishingly clear views of the universe have transformed our understanding of outer space. Its deployment in April 1990 marked a significant advancement in astronomy . . . some say it's the most significant development since Galileo's telescope back in 1610.

The Hubble Space Telescope is famous for snapping stunning photos of distant planets, stars, nebulae, and galaxies. The telescope does not actually travel to these places, but it takes pictures of them as it whirls around Earth at roughly 17,000 mph. Since it was launched, it has collected more than 50,000 images. The Hubble Space Telescope has had four servicing missions and has been operating for more than 25 years. Astronauts had to install new instruments and, in 1997, they extended the wavelength range so that scientists could probe the most distant reaches of the universe using the telescope.

HOW IT WORKS

The Hubble Space Telescope has six cameras and sensors that see visible, infrared, and UV light. Incoming light strikes the primary mirror and, through a hole in it, light is reflected onto the secondary mirror until it reaches science instruments. The telescope's primary mirror is roughly eight feet across, and the telescope itself is roughly 44 feet long—the length of a school bus! This complicated path of light increases the telescope's focal length, which provides exceptionally clear images.

Hubble's Breakthroughs

- The telescope helped astronomers determine the precise age for the universe, narrowing the universe's age to 13 to 14 billion years old.
- The photographs show the deepest views of the cosmos in visible, ultraviolet, and near-infrared light, uncovering evidence of black holes.

Images captured by the Hubble Space telescope

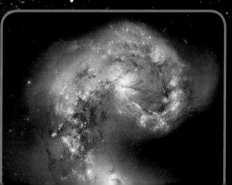

INTERNATIONAL SPACE STATION

The International Space Station (ISS) is a home and workplace for astronauts. It remains in low orbit around Earth for a long time. Space stations allow scientists to study many things in weightlessness or microgravity, including the effects of long-term spaceflight on the human body.

First launched in 1998 with many modules added over the years, the International Space Station was built so that astronauts from all over the world could visit and learn about space. A Russian rocket launched the first piece of ISS. Portions of the ISS were brought up into space one by one, mostly by Space Shuttle, and astronauts gradually assembled it like a puzzle. Two years later, the station was ready for people with the first crew arriving in 2000. NASA and its partners around the world finished the space station in 2011. Five different space agencies representing 15 countries built the 100-billion-dollar space station.

Its crew spends 35 hours a week conducting research to advance knowledge about Earth and space. A six-person crew typically stays for four to six months. Traveling 17,500 miles per hour, the ISS circles the globe every 90 minutes, seeing 15 or 16 sunrises and sunsets each day.

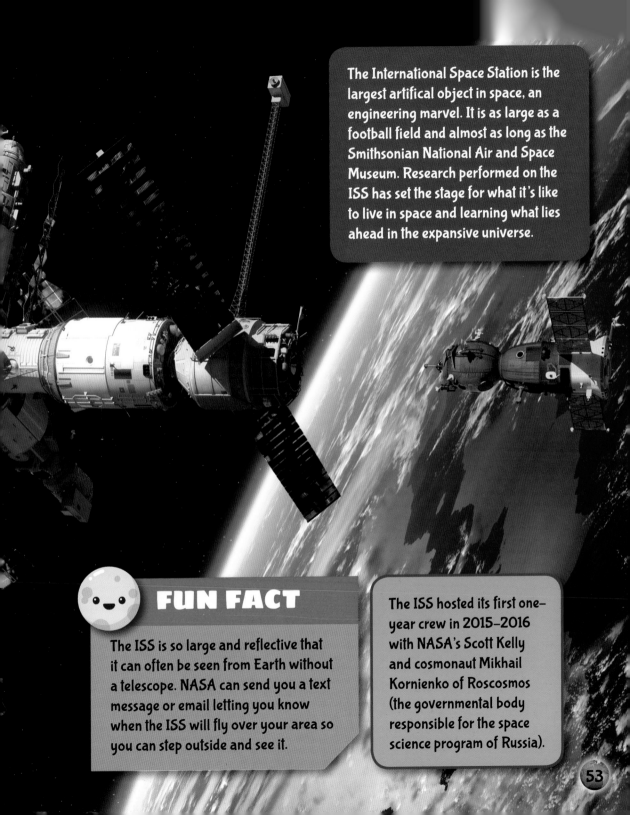

The International Space Station is the largest artifical object in space, an engineering marvel. It is as large as a football field and almost as long as the Smithsonian National Air and Space Museum. Research performed on the ISS has set the stage for what it's like to live in space and learning what lies ahead in the expansive universe.

FUN FACT

The ISS is so large and reflective that it can often be seen from Earth without a telescope. NASA can send you a text message or email letting you know when the ISS will fly over your area so you can step outside and see it.

The ISS hosted its first one-year crew in 2015–2016 with NASA's Scott Kelly and cosmonaut Mikhail Kornienko of Roscosmos (the governmental body responsible for the space science program of Russia).

GADGETS, ROCKETS, AND MORE!

So much of what has been explored and learned over time could not have been possible without the technological advancements that have happened in the last 500 years. Initially, all we knew about the universe was learned from the naked eye. Then Galileo took his telescope and pointed it to the skies. Since then, we have learned so much from telescopes, rovers, orbiters, rockets, and more!

Hubble's Album

The Hubble Space Telescope launched in 1990 and has taken many photographs of the planets in our solar system and some of the most distant objects in space. It has seen young stars forming and old stars dying. Its position above the atmosphere gives it a view of the universe that surpasses ground-based telescopes.

Galileo's Telescope

Galileo made his first telescope in 1609 but made modifications later on. Thanks to this telescope, Galileo was able to observe the Moon, discover Jupiter's moons and Saturn's rings, observe a supernova, and more.

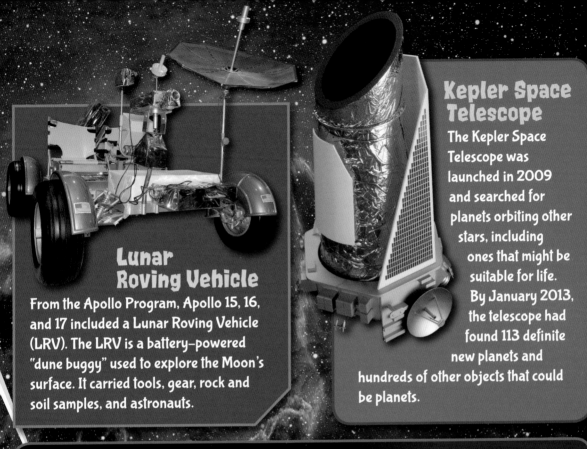

Kepler Space Telescope

The Kepler Space Telescope was launched in 2009 and searched for planets orbiting other stars, including ones that might be suitable for life. By January 2013, the telescope had found 113 definite new planets and hundreds of other objects that could be planets.

Lunar Roving Vehicle

From the Apollo Program, Apollo 15, 16, and 17 included a Lunar Roving Vehicle (LRV). The LRV is a battery-powered "dune buggy" used to explore the Moon's surface. It carried tools, gear, rock and soil samples, and astronauts.

Lunar Reconnaissance Order

Launched in June 2009, the Lunar Reconnaissance Order (LRO) is a robotic spacecraft that is orbiting around the Moon. LRO takes pictures of the Moon's surface. The goal of the LRO is to find safe landing sites on the Moon. NASA will use the information collected from LRO to create three-dimensional maps and measure how much radiation there is on the Moon. Another piece of equipment is studying the Moon's soil, searching for water near the moon's surface.

GADGETS, ROCKETS, AND MORE!

Orbiters

Orbiters have played a vital role in space exploration because they transport astronauts to and from space. Space Shuttles *Columbia*, *Challenger*, *Discovery*, *Atlantis*, and *Endeavor* all had orbiters that helped pave the way for the possibilities of space exploration.

Magellan

In 1989, a spacecraft called Magellan was launched from the Space Shuttle, and a little more than a year later it was orbiting Venus. It used radar to look through the planet's thick clouds and made a map of its surface. It found that Venus has thousands of volcanoes.

Saturn V Rocket

Launch vehicles are rockets that send things—and people—into space. Heavy-lift rockets are the most powerful. The Saturn V was a heavy-lift launch rocket. The rocket was built to send astronauts to the Moon. It was used in the Apollo program in the 1960s and 1970s. It was about as tall as a 36-story building . . . taller than the Statue of Liberty! Full of fuel, it weighed more than 3,000 tons. Three astronauts traveled in an Apollo spacecraft perched on top of the rocket. A total of 13 Saturn V rockets were launched between 1967 and 1973. The last one launched the first American space station, Skylab, and no one has built a bigger or more powerful rocket since.

SOYUZ SPACECRAFT

The *Soyuz* is a Russian spacecraft and it carries people and supplies, such as water and food, to and from the space station. The *Soyuz* is like a lifeboat . . . at least one *Soyuz* is always attached to the International Space Station and has room for three people to ride in it. If there was an emergency, the crew could use the *Soyuz* to return to Earth.

There are two parts to the *Soyuz*—the capsule and the rocket. The capsule is the orbital module. The crewmembers can live in the orbiter and connect to the space station. The rocket is what launches people and things into space. After launch, the rocket and the capsule separate. The rocket will return to Earth while the capsule continues into space.

WHAT'S NEXT?

MARS EXPLORATION

Mars rovers are robotic, automated motor vehicles that come equipped with cameras and a variety of tools and instruments for exploring. A robotic arm uses instruments to examine soil and rocks the way a geologist would.

Curiosity is a ten-foot-long, six-wheeled robot that landed on Mars in 2012. It took eight months to reach the planet from Earth. While exploring Mars's surface and gathering samples, *Curiosity* hopes to discover if there was ever life on Mars or if life on Mars could ever be possible.

Mars rover

CASSINI-HUYGENS

The Cassini–Huygens spacecraft is a joint effort between NASA, the European Space Agency, and the Italian Space Agency. It is packed with multiple, powerful instruments and cameras. It was launched with the Cassini orbiter and the Huygens probe. The Cassini was launched in 1997 and reached its destination, Saturn, in 2004. Since then, it has orbited the gas giant, taking amazing photos of Saturn's rings, moons, and weather. Once it reached Titan, Saturn's biggest moon, it descended to the moon via parachute to be the most distant spacecraft landing to date.

SHENZHOU 5

On October 15, 2003, China launched an astronaut into Earth's orbit with the *Shenzhou 5*, and became the third nation to successfully send a crewed spacecraft into space. China has since turned its focus to extraterrestrial exploration starting with the Moon. The Chinese Lunar Exploration Program sent a lunar orbiter, *Chang'e 1*, to the Moon becoming the fifth nation to successfully orbit the Moon. They also finished building the world's largest radio telescope, with a dish the size of 30 football fields, to scan for intelligent alien life.

WHAT'S NEXT?

NEW HORIZONS

The *New Horizons* mission was a nearly ten-year trip to reach Pluto. It was the first space exploration trip to the dwarf planet and ventured deep into the distant, mysterious Kuiper Belt. The probe is piano-sized and was launched in January 2006. By 2015, it was the closest to Pluto that scientists have ever gotten. As part of the mission, we learned about the surface properties, geology, and atmosphere on the dwarf planet. Scientists also learned that Pluto and its largest moon, Charon, are "ice dwarfs." They have solid surfaces, but, unlike the terrestrial planets, a portion of their mass is icy. *New Horizons* is now exploring how ice dwarf planets evolved over time.

SPACE X LANDS A ROCKET

Elon Musk and his private spaceflight company SpaceX made history in 2015. They brought the first stage of its Falcon 9 rocket back to Earth, which made history as the first-ever rocket landing during an orbital launch. SpaceX plans to develop reusable rockets as a way to open up space exploration in the future.

ONE-YEAR MISSION

In March 2015, American astronaut Scott Kelly and Russian cosmonaut Mikhail Kornienko partnered for their historic yearlong mission on the International Space Station. They resided on the ISS twice as long as a typical US mission. This mission acted as a stepping stone for future missions to Mars and showed how the two countries can collaborate in the future. While in space, they built the foundation for future six-month missions on the ISS and Mir. It also provided important information on how the human body adjusts to weightlessness, isolation, radiation, and stress of long-term spaceflight.

WHAT'S NEXT?

There is still so much of the universe to explore. Scientists and astronomers still have so many questions about other planets, our galactic neighbors, and more. Nearly every day, something new and exciting is happening and uncovered. Research is being done; studies lasting months and years are in progress.

Thanks to new technology such as these rockets, telescopes, orbiters, and capsules, astronauts, scientists, and astronomers are able to continue to explore the reaches of space that have yet to be explored and learn more about the planets, moons, and stars in our solar system. The sky isn't the limit for space exploration.

GLOSSARY

Galaxy: massive group of stars, planets, gas, and dust

Gravity: force of attraction between objects that depends on their mass

Heliosphere: region of space, encompassing the solar system, in which the solar wind has a significant influence

Mass: amount of matter in an object

Astronauts: people who are trained to live, work, and travel in a spacecraft in outer space

Astronomers: people who study stars, planets, comets, and asteroids

Atmosphere: the layer of gases surrounding a planet

Celestial: positioned in or relating to the sky; outer space as observed in astronomy

Orbit: path of a planet, moon, comet, or spacecraft around another body, such as a planet, moon, or star

Probe: un-piloted exploratory spacecraft designed to transmit information about its environment

Rovers: vehicles for driving over rough terrain, especially one driven by remote control over extraterrestrial terrain

Rocket: vehicle used to launch people and objects into space

Terrestrial: of, on, or relating to land

Solar system: group of planets, asteroids, comets, and moons that orbit a star. Our solar system is made up of eight planets (Mercury, Venus, Earth, Mars, Jupiter, Saturn, Uranus, and Neptune) and their moons, as well as asteroids and comets that orbit the Sun

Universe: all the space, matter, and energy in existence

ROCKET MODEL INSTRUCTIONS

1

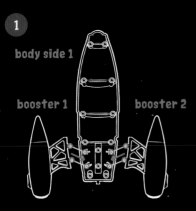

body side 1

booster 1   booster 2

Start with the half of the rocket body that has four plastic notches at the bottom. Fit the two boosters with plastic rings onto the notches.

2

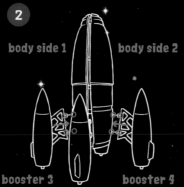

body side 1   body side 2

booster 3   booster 4

Join the two rocket halves, then attach the remaining boosters.

3

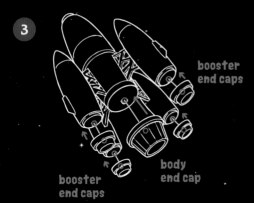

booster end caps

body end cap

booster end caps

Snap the four end caps onto the boosters, then press the body end cap to the underside of the rocket.

4

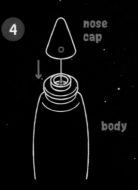

nose cap

body

Finally, connect the nose of the rocket.

finished model

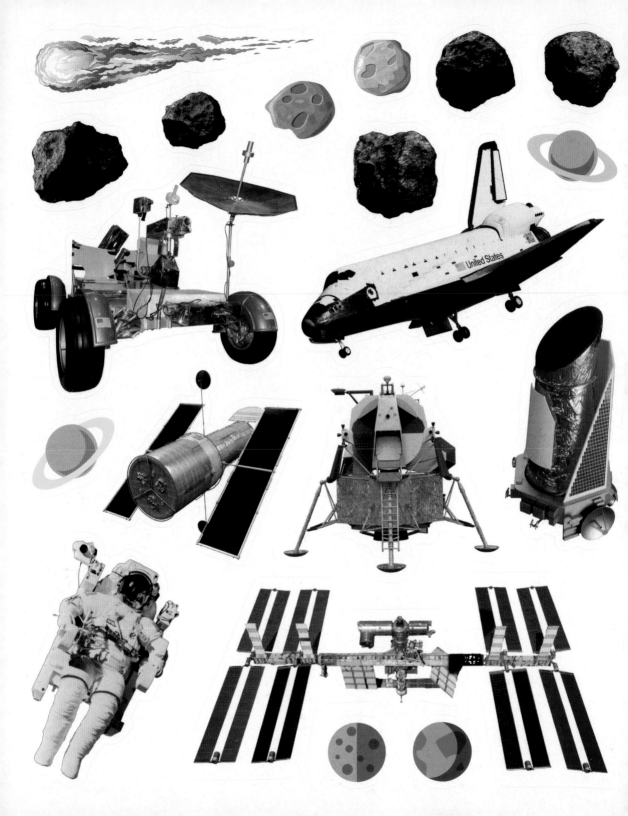

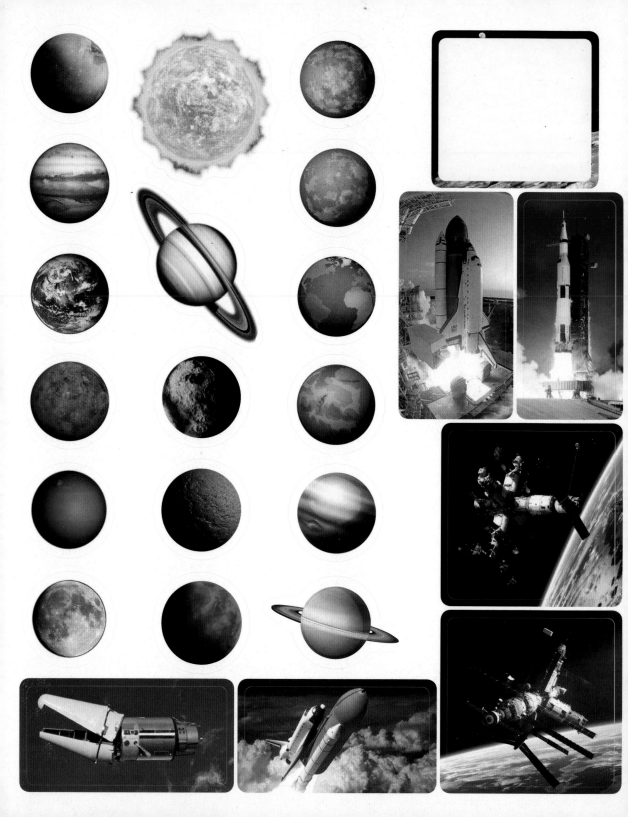

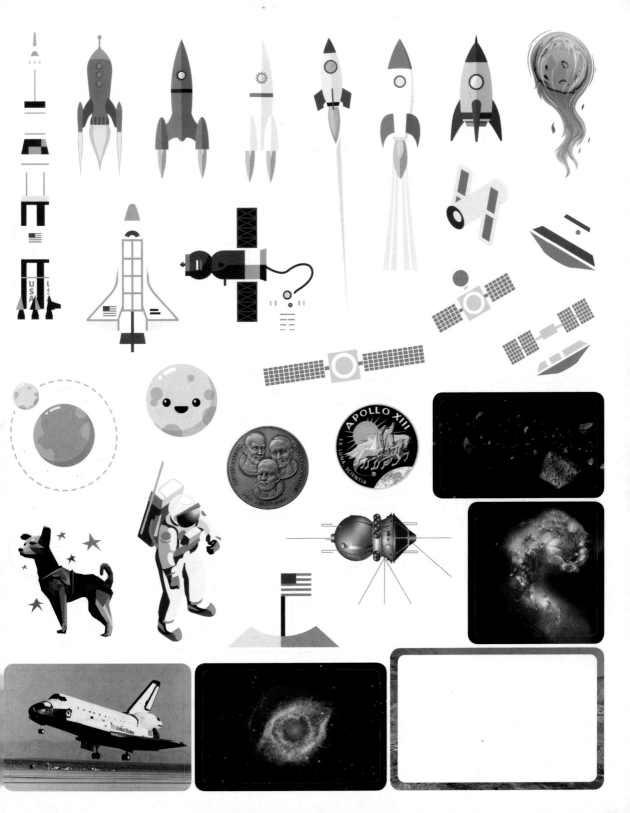